AF674279

Eunoia © 2022 Miley-Marie Bell

All rights reserved.

No part of this publication may be reproduced, stored in a retrieval system, or transmitted, in any form or by any means, electronic, mechanical, photocopying, recording or otherwise, without the prior written permission of the presenters.

Miley-Marie Bell asserts the moral right to be identified as author of this work.

Presentation by *BookLeaf Publishing*

Web: www.bookleafpub.com

E-mail: info@bookleafpub.com

ISBN: 9789357617161

First edition 2022

Eunoia

Miley-Marie Bell

BookLeaf Publishing

For all the people who gave me emotions both good and bad, I would have nothing to write about without you. And for my late Uncle Mark, because I keep my promises.

PREFACE

Dear readers,

This is my first venture into publishing my work and I am beyond excited to be able to share something I am so passionate about. Eunioa is the bond created between an author and their audience, it is the beautiful desire to share and to help and it is a bond like no other. I have been in love with literature for as long as I can remember. I taught myself to read when I was three, ask my mom she can confirm, and I've been writing since I could hold a pencil. I fell in love with the beauty of words. I went through a million dream jobs as a kid, everything from stunt pilot to scientist, but I always said I want to publish a book. I didn't think I would get to it while essentially a kid but here I am. I am so very thankful to the people reading these words, thank you for being my audience, thank you for allowing me to create this eunoia,

Miley-Maire

Little Midnight Gifts

Little midnight gifts, a glimpse of moonlight through the blinds, sweeping waves of cold air ready to whisk me away. Basking in the glow alone with my thoughts.

Peace despite the cold, despite the dark and the quiet noise of animals. My skin dappled with the soft haze, the shining blades of frosted grass diamonds for a time.

These are things that only in the sweetness of night do I see, only when it feels like I am the sole person to exist.

Small tokens for my tired eyes, I can not keep them,they can't even be held, but nonetheless they are there.

Deep in the dead of night I truly feel alive, every part of my body is more awake than ever, each fibre of my being feeling the moment.

Simple memories for me alone to hold, for no one's eyes but my own, my precious little midnight gifts.

Love me like a weed

Loving like a rose is overdone,
I've seen too many times that it has become boring.

Love me like the daisies we made crowns of as kids,
Make me feel as pretty as I did when a halo of them adored my head.

Love me like the bouquets of violets we picked,
Cherish me like we did those tiny little flowers.

Love me like the dandelions that made the lawn a sea of yellow,
Give me the same joy when I see you.

Love me like the flowers that took over the yard,
Do the same to my heart and mind.

Love me like the flowers we were allowed to pick,
The flowers adults deemed bad.

Love me the way we loved the bright coloured weeds as kids.

Expensive Candle

You want me to be an expensive candle, a soft light easy to put out and a gentle smell that only lasts a few hours. You want me to sit up on your highest shelf, out of your sight and mind but out of reach from those who truly want me. You make me wait until you want me again, for some reason I indulge you. On the rare nights you want me I am happy, I let you bask in the soft glow you make me provide. When you love me it is alone, just the two of us in the world you created and have convinced me is perfect. When you are bored of me you snuff me out and put me back up on that shelf, make me wait again.

We both know I am so much more.

I am a bonfire, I should be talked about, I am supposed to be celebrated. You should brag about me, dance and laugh around me. Enjoy my rich blinding light. I burn hot and fast, I am loud and angry but soft and caring. I should linger for months, engraved in your mind and suck in your senses. I am free in the open air, I am impossible to tame and you will never again confine me to your desolate room.

I am so much more than you want me to be, far more than you could ever handle. I cannot be dimmed and I refuse to be contained. I will never again be your expensive candle, I will remain a bonfire until my last coals burn out and I am reduced to nothing more than ash.

Old Stories

Time changes old stories,
That much is inevitable,
But why does it have to change what many hold most dear.

Why do ill fated lovers wither in to friends,
Why have victims become villains.

See myself

For a long time I couldn't see myself for what I was, it was scary so I denied it. When I finally accepted myself for what I am I couldn't see it around me so I didn’t tell a soul. Slowly I let people learn, learn to see me for who I am.

I became a collector, I collect the characters I relate to. Among the thousands upon thousands of pages I have, theirs are my favourite. They allow me to see myself, their ink and paper feel like home.

Pillow forts & Paper crowns

Kiss me in a pillow fort,
Make me a paper crown from rainbow sticky notes.

Let us build our own little kingdom,
One made of wool & fleece & love.

Our court jester will be a tv,
Cats & dogs will be our army,
Our loyal subjects will be teddy bears and dolls.

We will build a world where our love governs.

Nothing greater than a soulmate

Only the great die young,
This applies more to lovers than anyone else.

A great lover will die for you,
Without them the sun will seem to dissipate.

Simple mistakes will lead to tragedy,
Because nothing brings you joy like they did.

Soulmates are the death of themselves,
To them life is worth nothing without the other.

What we have

I do not wish to be liked by all,
I don't think I'm liked by many,
I just want you to be mine,
I just want to be yours.

I need nothing more than what we have.

Second hand poetry

There is a certain beauty to second hand poetry.

The spine broke at the page the stranger before you adored. Tear stains on the ones they cried over, pages dog-eared on the ones they wished to remember. Little notes left in their handwriting, these things seem so simple but all of these create a window into their mind.

The beauty of second hand poetry is getting to understand a stranger. Someone you've never met and probably never will. You no not their name nor their story but you know their mind.

Just the same

Everything is different,
Where we are,
What we look like,
Who we are with.

But everything is just the same,
Our love and the memories we have.

My beloved Ace,
We are still a team,
You are still my shoulder to cry on.

We left behind what hurt us,
And you still come running when I call.

Everything around us is different,
But what is most important,
The love we have for each other.
Is just the same.

Thoughts from 36,000 feet in the air

Bittersweet like coffee with sugar and cream,
Seeing homes that once were,
A life that once had been

Pavement tears fell on and people they fell for,
The walk I took home while dreaming of more

Places I was once a usual have long forgotten my name,
Shops have closed down but the city's heart remains the same

Streets act like veins,
Each person a cell,
There's so many I hope are still doing well

People never stop working,
I would never want them to,
I was just one person in their life,
A piece of the story just passing through

Home is so much more than one place,
It's found in feelings and memories,
A mixture of moments,
Each its own moment in time and in space

Beautiful Mistake

I want someone to make beautiful mistakes with.

Silly little things that don't mean much,
Stay out past curfew and get in shit because of it,
But it's worth it because of the memories we
made.

Someone to be reckless and impulsive with,
Because where you go I'll follow,
And I need someone to help me out of my
comfort zone.

Let's be stupid teens,
Dumb and in love.

We both know the odds are against us,
But we're still gonna try.

We will be fireworks,
Shooting for the stars,
Only to end up exploding in the sky.

Young love may be stupid and harsh,
It maybe asking for heartbreak,
But it's beautiful.

It’s bright and warm,
And if it is a mistake so be it,
Because it is a beautiful mistake to make.

Pretty

When you say pretty pictures are bound to come to mind,
Classically they are meadows of flowers,
Mountains glowing in the light of dawn.

I want to pretty like an abandoned building,
Slowly falling apart and messy and broken,
Yet somehow still endearing.

I want to be pretty like moss,
Simple and risillaint,
The base that helps things grow.

I want to be pretty like lightning,
Something people warn you of,
But you can't help but watch.

I want to be unconventionally pretty.

Pandora

Hope is the one thing that remains.

When fire was stolen from Olympus,
And the gods created Pandora.

When her curiosity got the better of her,
As she opened the jar they gave her.

When all the evil they created came flying out,
But she slammed the lid back down in a panic.

Hope is the one thing that remained,
So why does it seem so futile to hold on to it.

Notice

I want to notice.

I want to notice what makes you smile,
See the light flash in to your eyes,
The small curve of your lips.

I want no notice the lucky charm you always have,
I want to know where what it is,
I want to know why it's lucky.

I want to notice what makes you sad,
Even if you don't like showing it,
I want to notice the small changes in your face and voice.

I want to notice the things that take time,
The things no one else does.

Cemetery

I have always loved cemeteries,
The lines of carved stone,
Each the mark of a life.

Every person has a story,
They had a favourite colour and song,
They loved and lossed.

As weird as it sounds I have always been comfortable,
People say they like visitors.

Even though I've never known them maybe they do listen,
Maybe they read over my shoulder as I write,
Pouring parts of my own soul into the words.

The old overgrown ones are the nicest,
The stones chipped and crumbling,
Forgotten souls and stories happily waiting to be re-discovered.

Old souls seeing new life,
Someone so different from them.

Someone happily rambling about anything that comes to mind,
Not sure if anyone is even listening.

Sometimes it feels like someone sits down next to me,
But I rarely feel scared,
Maybe deep down I know they just want a friend.

Cemeteries have never been scary to me,
They are a library of the stories of lives.

Cliche

Let's be cliche.

Dance with me in the rain,
Learn to play my favourite songs,
Be there in all my best memories.

Tell me I'm a winner even when I loose,
Hold my hand just because you can,
Forever be my shoulder to cry on.

Let's be our own little rom-com,
Let's be cliche.

Sun & Moon

The sun & moon are said to be lovers,
Afterall opposites attract.

The sun is impossibly bright,
It's a giant ball of gas slowly burning up,
It's the ground and trees.

The moon is cold and soft,
It is solid and unwavering,
It is the ocean and the waves.

WIthout the sun we would not see the moon,
They like to show off their lover,
They are so far from each other it's the best the sun can do.

The moon takes care of the sun's creatures,
Gives them light in the dark,
Occasionally they get distracted by their lover's beauty.

The two of them are cursed to rarely be close,
On the miraculous times they are,
The moon is just fine to disappear.

We marvel at their love,
Study and record it,
For it is the eclipse,
For them it is a kiss.

Grey-Days

I have never liked grey-days.

Clouds accompanied not by wind and lightning,
But dread and a headache.

There is some dark magic to grey-days,
Not only the sky is grey,
It seems the entire world is.

Tolerance

When you are constantly in pain tolerance is natural,
Your body tries to help by making you numb.

Numb to nausea and needles,
And all the emotions that would usually come with it.

People are amazed with your tolerance and resilience,
But still question if it is really that bad.

Do us part

Don't let death do us part,
Wait for me beyond the grave,
Love me until the end of time,
And then some.

www.ingramcontent.com/pod-product-compliance
Lightning Source LLC
Chambersburg PA
CBHW062205160726
48282CB00027B/1006
9789357617161